The Australian
Bahá'í House of Worship

Set within natural bushland, it is one of the most beautiful and tranquil places to visit in Sydney.

Produced and Published by Simon Creedy

© 2025 Copyright - The National Spiritual Assembly of the Bahá'ís of Australia (www.bahai.org.au)

The Greatest Name Symbol

The symbol known as 'The Greatest Name' is a calligraphic rendering of Yá Bahá'u'l-Abhá and is positioned at the centre of the dome.

The symbol is used by Bahá'ís as a distinctive mark of the Cause of God and is an invocation which means 'O Glory of the All Glorious!' The word 'Bahá', or 'Glory', is a reference to Bahá'u'lláh.

The Australian Bahá'í House of Worship

173 Mona Vale Road, Ingleside, NSW 2101

THE AUSTRALIAN BAHÁ'Í HOUSE OF WORSHIP

- 1   A Brief Introduction
- 4   The Bahá'í Faith in Australia
- 6   The Australian Bahá'í House of Worship
- 8   Prayer - Blessed is the Spot - by Bahá'u'lláh
- 9 - 23   Illustrations of the Bahá'í House of Worship in Early Spring
- 24   The Central Figures of the Bahá'í Faith
- 26   Some Bahá'í Principles
- 27   Who are the Bahá'ís

Bahá'u'lláh designated the Bahá'í House of Worship as a spiritual gathering place for prayers and meditation around which will cluster social, humanitarian, educational and scientific institutions.

"...it forgeth bonds of unity from heart to heart; it is a collective centre for men's souls."

– 'Abdu'l-Bahá

A Brief Introduction

The Sydney Bahá'í House of Worship also known as the Bahá'í Temple is a foremost destination for anyone seeking spiritual enrichment and a deeper connection, offering an unforgettable experience that is nourishing for both the soul and the spirit.

People often feel a sense of warmth and unity because this Temple is dedicated to bringing people of all Faiths and backgrounds together in a spirit of love and harmony.

You will be welcomed whether you are a member of the Bahá'í community, simply a visitor or someone interested to learn more about the Bahá'í Faith.

In the early 1950s, the Bahá'ís of Sydney were supported by the worldwide Bahá'í community to undertake the construction of a House of Worship.

Despite facing challenges along the way, the community persevered and created something truly special.

Today, the Temple represents a beacon of hope and unity, attracting visitors from all over the world.

As you explore the grounds, you will discover beautiful gardens filled with native Australian flora, a visitors' centre, a bookshop and a picnic area where you can relax and enjoy the tranquillity.

Every week, the House of Worship welcomes a vibrant community to come together in prayer and fellowship.

At the public service held every Sunday and on special occasions, you will hear prayers and readings from the holy writings of all the major world religions and experience the heavenly voices of the a cappella choir, lifting your heart and nourishing your soul.

The Baháʼí Faith in Australia

The history of the Baháʼí Faith in Australia began in 1920 with the arrival of John Henry Hyde Dunn and Clara Dunn to Sydney.

Hyde Dunn (1855-1941) was an Englishman and Clara Dunn (1869-1960) was raised in Canada by Irish parents. Both had become Baháʼís in the United States in the early twentieth century.

The First Baháʼís

Clara and Hyde Dunn were a devoted couple who dedicated their lives to introducing the Baháʼí Faith to their new friends in Australia and New Zealand. With unwavering enthusiasm, they travelled extensively, sharing the teachings of Baháʼu'lláh with everyone they met.

Hyde Dunn, born in London in 1855, discovered the Baháʼí Faith in Seattle in 1905. He was deeply moved by the words of Baháʼu'lláh and became a passionate advocate for the Faith. Clara, born in Ireland in 1869, became a Baháʼí in Walla Walla, Washington and met Hyde in 1907. They married in 1917 and formed a dynamic partnership in sharing the Baháʼí message.

The Dunns were deeply inspired by ʻAbdu'l-Bahá during His visit to California in 1912, when He called for pioneers to travel to new lands. The Dunns responded with eagerness, despite their limited funds.

In 1920, they arrived in Sydney and began their remarkable journey, travelling throughout Australia and New Zealand and sharing the Bahá'í teachings with others.

Hyde, who travelled extensively for work, was able to share the teachings of the Bahá'í Faith widely. Clara's compassionate nature drew people to her, and together they established several Bahá'í communities and played a crucial role in forming the first National Spiritual Assembly of the Bahá'ís of Australia and New Zealand.

After Hyde's passing in 1941, Clara continued to serve the Bahá'í community with unwavering dedication, travelling and speaking extensively. Her appointment as a Hand of the Cause in 1952 recognized her tireless efforts, and she remained a beloved figure in the Bahá'í community until her passing in Sydney in 1960.

An amazing journey

The Bahá'í House of Worship was officially opened in 1961.

As the country welcomed more immigrants after World War II, the community grew and became more diverse. First Nations people, like Uncle Fred Murray, were among the first to join.

In the 1960s and 70s, the community welcomed new members who were drawn to the Bahá'í focus on peace and unity. In the 1980s, Bahá'ís fleeing persecution in Iran, whose stories of resilience and contribution are truly inspiring, found a safe haven in Australia.

Today, there are Bahá'ís in every city and regional area of Australia, who are working together to create a vibrant community through service and education.

The Bahá'í community is partnering with like-minded organisations to work towards common goals like equality, peace and human rights.

The Australian Bahá'í House of Worship

The House of Worship or Mashriqu'l-Adhkár meaning: *"The Dawning place of the praise of God"* is a special place created by Bahá'u'lláh where people of all Faiths and backgrounds can come together to pray and connect with their Creator.

The Bahá'í House of Worship is a central part of Bahá'í community life, bringing together prayer and service.

When Bahá'ís in Iran faced persecution in 1955, they were denied the possibility to build a House of Worship in Tehran. As a result the Guardian of the Bahá'í Faith, Shoghi Effendi, decided to build two Houses of Worship instead - one in Kampala, Uganda and the other in Sydney, Australia.

In February 1956, a seven-acre site was purchased in Ingleside, for the construction of the Bahá'í House of Worship. The plans were officially unveiled at the 1957 Bahá'í National Convention. Funds were raised from Australian and international Bahá'í communities, and after a four-year construction period, the stunning nine-sided temple was dedicated in September 1961.

The Temple's construction sparked widespread public interest, with The Brisbane Telegraph reporting on January 17, 1958, "THE BAHÁ'ÍS BUILD A CHURCH." The article described the £150,000 project as a future centre for a hospital, school and college, making it a hub for spiritual, cultural, educational and welfare activities.

The Lord Mayor of Sydney hosted a reception for international dignitaries attending the dedication. The event received extensive press coverage, including a report by The Daily Telegraph on September 18, highlighting the presence of 100 visitors from 20 countries among the 1,800 attendees. Church newspapers and international magazines like Time and The Economist also published articles about the Temple.

Notably, the persecution of Bahá'ís in Iran led to the construction of the Sydney Temple and accelerated the migration of Persian Bahá'ís to Australia and New Zealand, although the 1979 Islamic Revolution led to a more significant influx.

The construction of the Australian Bahá'í House of Worship in 1960

The Construction 1957 - 61

In 1957, the Bahá'ís of Australia undertook an ambitious project to build a Temple in Sydney, which was completed in over 4 years and has become a symbol of unity and oneness. The project was funded entirely by donations from the Bahá'í community.

Designed by the esteemed architect John Brogan, the Temple's innovative construction process and breathtaking design made it an instant icon, renowned for its original and stunning architecture.

The construction process was ground breaking, featuring inventive techniques such as the use of a helicopter to place the prefabricated lantern structure atop the dome – a first in Australia, which attracted significant media attention.

Upon completion, a ceremonial plate bearing the Arabic inscription "O Glory of the All Glorious" was placed at the dome's centre. The Temple was formally dedicated and opened to the public on September 17, 1961.

Today, this striking 38 meter high and 30 meter diameter Temple stands as a prominent landmark on Sydney's Northern Beaches, showcasing its unique design and spiritual significance.

Blessed is the spot,
and the house,
and the place,
and the city,
and the heart,
and the mountain,
and the refuge,
and the cave,
and the valley,
and the land,
and the sea,
and the island,
and the meadow
where mention of God
hath been made,
and His praise
glorified.

Bahá'u'lláh

A GLIMPSE THROUGH THE TREES

The Central Figures of the Bahá'í Faith

Bahá'u'lláh

Bahá'u'lláh (1817-1892), the Prophet-Founder of the Bahá'í Faith, proclaimed Himself to be the latest in a line of Divine Messengers, heralding a new era of spiritual enlightenment. His teachings emphasize the unity of God, the inter-connectedness of all major religions, and the oneness of humanity.

Bahá'u'lláh endured 40 years of torture, imprisonment and exile. His message of love and unity has inspired countless individuals worldwide.

The Báb

The Báb (1819-1850), meaning "the Gate", was the Forerunner of Bahá'u'lláh, preparing the way for His coming.

The Báb's declaration of His mission in 1844 sparked a wave of persecution, culminating in His martyrdom and the execution of over 20,000 of His followers.

'Abdu'l-Bahá

'Abdu'l-Bahá (1844-1921) the eldest son of Bahá'u'lláh was known for His advocacy of social justice and international peace. After His father's passing, 'Abdu'l-Bahá became the Head of the Faith, the authorized interpreter and the perfect Exemplar of Bahá'u'lláh's teachings.

'Abdu'l-Bahá spent His life promoting peace, unity and social renewal, establishing local institutions and guiding various initiatives.

Following His release from imprisonment, He travelled extensively throughout Europe and North America, sharing His Father's teachings and inspiring spiritual and social transformation.

Shoghi Effendi

'Abdu'l-Bahá appointed Shoghi Effendi (1897-1957) as the Guardian of the Bahá'í Faith, guiding the community through a period of significant transition. With unrelenting passion and dedication, Shoghi Effendi served as the Guardian from 1921 to 1957. His visionary leadership and guidance played a crucial role in shaping the community's growth and maturation during a transformative era.

The Universal House of Justice

The Universal House of Justice is the supreme governing body of the Bahá'í Faith, responsible for guiding and administering the global Bahá'í community.

Established in 1963, it is an international council of nine members elected every five years. The Universal House of Justice makes decisions on matters of policy, and administration, translating into reality Bahá'u'lláh's vision for a spiritually and materially prosperous global civilisation and promoting the unity and growth of the Bahá'í community worldwide. Its headquarters are located at the Bahá'í World Centre in Haifa, Israel.

The Universal House of Justice plays a central role in the Bahá'í Faith, ensuring the Faith's integrity and progress while fostering global cooperation and understanding.

"...The fact that he is by origin a Jew or a Christian, a black man or a white man, is not important anymore, but, as you say, lends colour and charm to the Bahá'í community in that it demonstrates unity in diversity."

– Shoghi Effendi

Some Bahá'í Principles

Oneness of God

Oneness of humanity

Common foundation of all religions

Universal peace upheld by a world government

Independent investigation of truth

Essential harmony of science and religion

Equality of men and women

Elimination of prejudice of all kinds

Elimination of extremes of wealth and poverty

Universal compulsory education

Spiritual solution to economic problems

Universal auxiliary language

Peaceful gardens and bushland surround the Bahá'í House of Worship, perfect for quiet reflection and prayer.

WHO ARE THE BAHÁ'ÍS?

Welcome to the Bahá'í Faith, a global family united by a shared vision of a harmonious world!

Bahá'ís believe in Bahá'u'lláh, The Manifestation of God for today whose teachings aim to create a harmonious, just and peaceful world, fostering spiritual growth, social progress and global unity.

Bahá'ís are dedicated to fostering spiritual growth and unity in ourselves, our communities, our nation and the world.

Through daily practices like prayer, study, meditation and service we strive to align our thoughts and actions with our spiritual values. We collaborate with others to create neighbourhood activities that uplift, support and bring together diverse groups, building vibrant and harmonious communities.

These initiatives include devotional gatherings that nurture spiritual well-being, children's classes that teach virtues and values and study circles that explore life's fundamental questions and spiritual principles. Youth are integral to all aspects of community life, playing a vital role in shaping a brighter future for all.

A community prayer meeting held at a local park

www.ingramcontent.com/pod-product-compliance
Lightning Source LLC
Chambersburg PA
CBRC102341090526
44590CB00010B/152